EARTH GIANT TREE GIFT SERIES – BOOK 5

Olive Tree's Gift

ROCHELLE HEVEREN

 TREE VOICE PUBLISHING

Earth Giant Tree Gift Series: Olive Tree's Gift

TREE VOICE PUBLISHING PTY LTD
ACN. 627 784 294 ABN . 94627784294
4 Wirreanda Court Blackburn Victoria 3130 AUSTRALIA
Phone +613 9878 4600
Email: hello@treevoice.global
www.treevoice.global

First published in 2019
Copyright text © Rochelle Heveren
Copyright © Tree Voice Publishing

www.facebook.com/TreeVoiceAuthor
www.facebook.com/RochelleHeverenAuthor
Instagram: @treevoiceglobal
Instagram: @rochelle_with_love_x

All rights reserved. No part of this publication may be reproduced in whole or in part, stored in a retrievable system, or transmitted in any form or by any means, electronic, mechanical, photocopying, recording or otherwise, without written permission of the copyright holder or publisher.

Designed by Tree Voice Publishing Pty Ltd
Printed by Ingram Spark
ISBN: 978-0-6483912-6-5 (paperback)

 A catalogue record for this book is available from the National Library of Australia

*I know with my whole being,
that when I sit and a tree connects,
that it is never just for me.*

*This little book
has BIG heart and soul.*

*My commitment to share this with you,
my friend, is promised.*

– Love Rochelle xxx

Sitting at the base of my new friend Olive in Olympus, Greece I feel a surge of strength, determination and perseverance infuse my being.

I feel encouraged to live my life with a newfound confidence. This immediately silences my doubts and inability to be myself. I can finally just be 'me'.

Foreword

Olive Tree's Gift is the channelled teachings of one of Earth's great Masters. This wise being, over two thousand year old, will bring you strength, determination, perseverance and confidence – a unique way of guiding life's journey. He'll remind you of the importance of facing what stands in your way, waking an inner strength and determination to regain who you really want to be. Through perseverance, a new confidence will strip away self-doubt and worry. Olive will ignite your passion, purpose and true inner knowing.

Being supported with the magic of *Olive Tree's Gift* is like resting your back against his trunk and listening to his whispers of great wisdom. Allow his words to encourage you with love.

This inspiring gift book is designed to unlock your own heart's wisdom. Rochelle invites you to discover the magic, strength and newfound confidence that she experienced, sitting and resting her back against the Olive tree in Olympus, Greece.

Written in Olympus, Greece

Contents

Introduction 1

Chapter 1: Meeting My New Friend 7

Chapter 2: Infusing a Newfound Confidence 12

Chapter 3: Perseverance over Obstacles 16

Chapter 4: Confidence 23

Chapter 5: Passion or Obsession 27

Chapter 6: Passion Fires Up 32

Chapter 7: Space Held for Loss 37

Chapter 8: Commitment 41

Chapter 9: Dilution of Purpose 44

Chapter 10: Breaking Old Habits 47

Chapter 11: Embracing Change 52

Introduction

My adventure begins as I travel through Italy. I visit many family vineyards where I gorge on feasts of passionately-prepared Italian pasta accompanied by abundant bottles of wine. After one of these winery feasts I stop at the Eiffel Tower in Pisa. The Eiffel Tower seems almost upright in my tipsy state!

One night in Rome, I laugh and get swept up in the talent of a comical opera. The next day I climb many flights of stairs and descend into tunnels to find the ancient history discovered beneath Rome. I discover that, like lasagne, this city has been layered and built on top of itself over time. In Rome I also hear stories of battles of human spirit, and even those of animals, lost and won in the Colosseum.

In awe, I view many of Michelangelo's masterpieces. His gift for sculpting from large slabs of stone is incredible. I stand and admire the effort in bringing his statue of David to life.

I feel instant pride in the Italians I meet. Whenever I sit in a restaurant I feel like a visitor in their home. I witness extreme happiness on their faces if I leave my plate spotless at the end of a meal – this is seen as a compliment to the chef. I am offered a small glass of Limoncello at the end of my meal, particularly if I've eaten it all. Wine and more wine highlights the romantic destinations I visit, and I enjoy a gondola trip through the canal city of Venice.

I travel down the Amalfi. This coastal road is tight and narrow, and the driver displays extreme patience and skill as he drives only millimetres from the other cars, vans and buses travelling in the opposite direction. By boat I travel out of Sorrento to Capri, where I marvel over the deep turquoise water. I cannot resist taking a swim.

My trip is rich in history.

Across the bay I fly to Athens. Greece feels immediately different from Italy. The many metropolises I visit are bursting with ancient ruins. I feel Greece to be drier and less abundant than Italy, which was filled with trees and greenery.

I adore the Greek food. Rather than Limoncello, I am now offered Ouzo. Ouzo is considered a great digestive and is drunk straight up at the start of a meal. I enjoy liquorice, so appreciate this tradition. The saganaki – grilled cheese with tzatziki dip – becomes a favourite and I order it with almost every meal. There is no limit to the food and drink on which I gorge while I immerse myself in the Greek traditions.

In Athens I learn of the invasions in Greece. War tore Greece apart, resulting in many families fleeing their homes and spreading out across the world. I am surprised to learn that one-third of the largest community of Greeks today lives in my hometown of Melbourne, Australia.

I join a four-day tour that takes me to more ancient ruins. I visit many old cities of stone columns and pathways that lead up hilltops that were once bustling metropolises. The Greeks' love of sport and competition is evident among these ruins. There is always a stadium for races and competition. Each stadium is set up for many spectators, with tiered stone seating around the edges.

When I arrive in Olympus, I feel a shift and stirring in my being. I discover that as well as Mount Olympus being the highest mountain in Greece, it's the most picturesque site. Due to this majesty, remoteness and beauty, it was only natural for the Ancient Greeks to believe this to be the home of their most important gods. It was from Olympus that the twelve principal gods, the Olympians, presided over the world: Zeus, the king of the gods; his wife, Hera; his brothers, Poseidon and Hades; his sisters, Demeter and Hestia; and his children, Apollo, Artemis, Ares, Aphrodite, Athena, Hermes and Hephaestus. These Olympian gods and goddesses were archetypes, representing idealized aspects of the multi-faceted human psyche.

It was by worshipping each of the deities that that particular aspect of behaviour and personality was invoked and amplified in the worshipper.

Zeus was the god of mind and intellect, and a protector of strangers. Hera was the goddess of fertility, along with the stages of a woman's life and marriage. Apollo represented law and order, being moral, social and intelligent. Aphrodite was the goddess of love and passion. Hermes was the god of the travellers, sleep and dream prophecy. Athena represented spiritual wisdom. Hephaestus was the god of the arts and fire. Ares represented the dark, bloodthirsty aspects of human nature.

The ancient myths served as metaphors for the power of the sacred mountain.

I learn that the Olympian gods once overthrew the Titans during the legendary Battle of the Titans, before placing their divine kingdom there.

This spiritual power drew many hermits and monks to live in the caves and forests in Olympus, long before the Christians came. When Christianity arrived, the myths and legends of the old Greeks were suppressed and forgotten.

My accommodation is atop a mountain bursting with greenery. Old, winding streets pass the homes filled with olden-day charm and character. It isn't just because of the myths and legends that this place represents, that my heart feels a stirring. I feel awake and filled with an inner knowledge that I will meet someone really special when I visit the birthplace of the Olympic Games.

When I arrive at the grounds of the Olympics, I notice the gardens bursting abundantly with ancient trees, breathtakingly beautiful. Walking around the grounds, I see where the first races were held and where the heavy balls of lead and long javelins were thrown. I feel alive and my energy instantly lifts. I imagine how the many athletes must have also felt when they arrived here.

I explore the old stone gymnasium, the stadium and remnants of old temples, and also wander through the grounds. There are many olive trees here, almost unrecognisable because they are so overgrown and not the usual shape I'm accustomed to seeing. They haven't been maintained or trimmed back, so picking the olives is easy. Many of the trees are huge, towering over 20 metres in the air; overgrown giants with thick, gnarly trunks, with deep crevices of history wrinkling their form. It's only when I see olives hanging high up in the branches that I know for sure that these are olive trees. I imagine they were planted for many reasons, particularly to provide branches to twist into crowns for the winners of the Olympics Games.

CHAPTER 1

Meeting My New Friend

As I walk around Olympus, I feel a gentle pull towards several trees I pass. Beside the old gymnasium is a very old and stunning olive tree. I reach out my hand and place it onto her bark, feeling her female energy of encouragement. I walk a little further into the grounds and down beside the temple of Zeus. Unusually there is no rope dividing the path, so I walk in and around the old ruins.

There are massive boulders of stone, overgrown with ivy and surrounded by long grass. I walk between these boulders that are remnant columns. I'm amazed that they date back as far as 4000 BC.

Then I suddenly stop. Before me stands a gigantic tree. Because it is so overgrown, at first I'm unsure what type it is. Vines hug some of its trunk and then wind up through the branches above. Over a metre wide, the trunk is solid with old, gnarly knots etched into the thick bark. I'm intrigued and enthralled by a feeling of great empowerment as I stand here. Spotting tiny olives up in the branches, I realise this giant is an olive tree. He is simply huge.

Holding my hand firmly on his trunk I look up into his massive canopy. I'm grateful to stand under his shade in today's scorching sun.

I take three breaths into my heart, my soul connection to Olive, to stop my thoughts getting in the way. I smile and say, "Good morning…"

I hear a strong male voice: "Your trip long – welcome."

It is like he was waiting for me. I feel happy that I've chosen this olive tree.

"I feel honoured that you welcome me, and am excited to meet someone planted with purpose; I imagine not just for the fruit you bear."

"Yes, from my branches was twisted a winning crown," Olive responds.

Our conversation is so easy.

"How old are you?" I ask, thinking if he were

human he may be offended by my question. "Did you experience the birth of what today we call the Olympics?"

"Pushed into earth with purpose, I symbolised determination, perseverance and eventually someone's reach for a crown in victory." Olive's words are poetic.

I love that my new friend is male.

"Can you please tell me about the athletes that may have rested here in your shade?" I'm desperate to hear more.

"Years passed before I shaded. When I did, just as you have done today, I threaded and connected into their spirits. I saw their hopes and dreams. I could see their personal sacrifice in standing out, in competing and being different from normal people back then. Their ordinary lives were abandoned. Instead, they set disciplines to push themselves further. Run faster, throw further and leap higher."

I'm shown a vision of the athletes in action as they train around these grounds. Occasionally they rest beneath nearby trees before pushing themselves further. What I see is tough, a sacrifice.

"What can you tell me about the difference between those who won in competition and those who were runners up?"

"It was belief," Olive says, pausing, before explaining further. "Without self-belief, nothing is possible. As soon as comparisons or self-doubt entered their minds, they were defeated instantly."

I nod my head and consider that this is spot-on, not just in terms of athletic feats, but with anything in life. Giving up before starting – or starting and then stopping because of thoughts of not being good enough – diminishes any hope of winning.

"When a winner sat beneath and against you, what is the one thing that stood out to you?" I ask Olive.

"Winners never compete against others. They push to be faster than themselves. They are gratified by their own personal feat. A real winner is someone who lives without ego and praise. My favourite athlete was the humble winner."

"Thank you for your insight, for opening this doorway back in time to this part of history. I also want to express gratitude for your shade during the heat of today's sun here in Greece." I drink deeply from my water bottle.

I'm in no hurry to leave and love where I'm sitting, soaking in Olive's positive, uplifting vibe.

I commend the athletes from long ago for being the first to participate in something new. I also congratulate them in their ability to win a competition. They were champions because of their perseverance, determination and drive. The winners had a personal commitment to being their own best, inspired to compete by other athletes' abilities.

I then change the subject. "I love that you are a male tree. Can I visit you again and feel you thread new lessons within my understanding and way of being?"

"The threading is done. I'm honoured you chose me. I know you were also drawn to my sister Olive by the gymnasium. I look forward to working with you." Olive rustles his outer branches.

I smile. I'm excited about insights to come. When I make such a deep connection with a tree-friend, a series of lessons and gifts unfolds. I am excited about the journey that awaits with Olive. I don't imagine being an athlete myself, so I wonder what Olive can help me with right now in my life.

CHAPTER 2

Infusing a Newfound Confidence

Our conversation continues. "I know that you're connected to all the olive trees globally. I've travelled throughout Morocco and Egypt and I've noticed that in the Middle East, olives are used as part of the staple diet. There are groves of olive trees all over the world, even back home in Australia. Can you share with me the gift your tree brings to our world?" I ask curiously.

"Far and wide, for spiritual reasons as well as nutritional ones, the olive is revered as a tree of life," Olive tells me.

I remember being taught biblical stories as a young girl about a dove flying into the ark, holding an olive branch in its beak. This was a sign that the floods had stopped and new life was now growing. The olive branch was a symbol of peace.

In Morocco, I loved the fact that olives were offered to us at every meal. Olive oil sits beside my stovetop at home and I use it in my cooking most days.

"What else can you share about olive trees?" I press for more.

"To lay or rest your back against me or one of my family always infuses strength from Olive into you. Eating olives or using the oil in cooking gives strength to your constitution. Emotionally, physically and mentally you become stronger by having me in your life. In history the oil of olive was often used to anoint. Human minds were instantly cleared by this anointment."

I'm happy that I love the taste of olives. I smile, knowing I have already gained some of the benefits of olives in my life.

Since being threaded and connected to Olive, I have felt an instant and obvious shift in my confidence. I feel like someone has vacuumed away all my previous doubts. It's like I've become more aligned in my mind.

"You know, you have changed me already," I tell my friend. "What I mean is once not feeling strong enough to speak up even though I wanted to do so. Now I'm beginning to trust my instincts more. As a teenager and young adult, I was more like this. Actually, I was more like this until my childhood memories crashed through in my early 30s."

I become silent as my mind takes me back to a feeling of utter uselessness. Post-natal depression debilitated me for many years as a mother with four young children. At that time, even the simplest task became overwhelming. Since my early 30s, I have never regained my previous strength and confidence. I lacked self-belief and always second-guessed everything I said and did. I'm sure I drove those closest in my life crazy with my constant neediness and questioning.

Now I feel like the shift Olive has made within me is shaken awake.

My thoughts are interrupted as Olive begins to speak: "You have always had strength and determination. These things were just choked by old, learned patterns. These old ways of being held you for ransom. Programmed ways were part of your life as a young girl, when you learned the fear of making the wrong choice. As a child, this led to you being taken from and broken. You realised that it was safer to ask what to do, and so you became controlled by the need to please others. Most of the world is programmed by the need of praise from others."

My mind turns to social media. How many times have I started to post something important to me, but then stopped in fear of judgement? Sometimes I've written on others' posts before then deleting my comments, for the same reason.

"Just sitting here, I feel more confident to share authentically with others. I no longer feel driven to always try to clarify what to do next. I hope that this shift in my own energy will now ripple out to everyone with whom I connect."

"Go and share the fact that everyone has strength and determination. When this is harnessed, everyone can live lives full of confidence. This is a big part of authenticity, you know?"

Olive is right. As soon as I feel strength and determination, I immediately feel confidence as well. It is time to honour my own belief in myself.

CHAPTER 3

Perseverance over Obstacles

My attention is drawn to the ivy that has wound its way across most of the area around Olive. Ivy covers a large circle stone that stands upright on its side. It looks pretty. I notice that ivy has also travelled up the trunk of my friend, all the way up to where the branches spread out high and wide.

There are many big slabs of stone in this area, and I notice that one leans against Olive's base. I guess that over time the strength of Olive's growth has pushed and lifted this obstacle.

The walls and structure of the temple of Zeus were discarded and rocked free when the earthquake destroyed the main structure many years ago. Olive stands beside the temple of Zeus. It is incredible that over time Olive lifted this stone with his strength and growth.

"So much strength you must have exerted to lift this massive slab," I say.

"Inner strength and endurance can shift anything. Bit by bit, this stone didn't stand in my way," Olive responds proudly.

"Can we talk about how you shifted such a heavy stone?" I ask.

"There are always at least two choices in life — to push forward or simply give up. With all my strength, bit by bit I never allowed anything to get in the way of my growth. I lifted this obstacle you refer to with my own perseverance. Now that I am threaded to you, I notice that there have been some things you walked away from but at other times you have persevered."

I instantly think of when I first picked up my pen and trusted the words that flowed, about five years ago now. I knew I had to bring the messages of the trees into the world, even though at times I'd come close to giving up. Some obstacles blocked me but I found strength from within to push forward, in spite of anything I thought might stop me. In the end I haven't been stopped.

"I was once told that if there is a block or

something difficult, it is a sign to walk away. Yet deep within, if I felt really passionate about something and encountered an obstacle, I found more strength to make change happen. My writing is a good example of this." I try to relay to Olive that I understand what he means.

"Never give up when it comes to your purpose. Your heart's passion and goals are always worth the effort – therefore your growth will push aside anything that gets in the way."

There's a quiet space of reflection before Olive continues: "The human race has permitted excuses. Too tired, bored, sad, unworthy... and so the list goes on. It's time for your inner strength to be supported in your life. If you really want a positive outcome, then push forward. But do this gently, because it's never a war or battle. Waking up your inner endurance and perseverance will eventually get results."

I move to sit on the ground beside the slab of stone Olive lifted. I am still under the shade of Olive. I feel a rush of his pure energy charge through me. Any doubts and fears of not being 'enough', dissolve. I feel confident, filled with an inner strength within that had once been dormant. I do deserve all that

I've worked for! I feel the enormity of strength from my friend – the strength taken to shift the weight of such a huge stone. Once more I soak up the feeling of Olive's commitment, determination and confidence.

"Wow, I've never felt anything like this, except when I gave birth to my babies." I smile lovingly as I think of that magical time. I totally understand what Olive is showing me. It seemed impossible to bring a baby in my belly into the world. It took effort, determination and a complete desire to birth. This is the sort of strength that Olive wants me to tap into.

"Yes, that strength. Draw on that strength to make your goals possible," Olive affirms.

It is a matter of giving everything I have.

"Thank you, Olive." I let out a sigh. "You have woken me. Something I've lost is now revived."

I feel my fire of purpose re-ignited.

"Is there anything else you tell me about overcoming obstacles?"

"An obstacle only exists when you give up. It isn't in your way if you don't accept defeat."

I think of the athletes who competed here and

also of the difficulties within my own life. I consider Olive's words. Does overcoming a block have something to do with perspective? Can someone create different outcomes depending on whether they choose to give everything to change a difficult situation, or just give up? I imagine this is true. Years ago I could have just accepted my shortcomings and never tried to be a better 'me'.

"Never fear a difficult time. It is an opportunity to figure out a new way." Olive is kind, yet direct.

I think of the great efforts I have made to stay connected to my once shut-down heart. In the end, through perseverance, my encased heart was cracked open. Without effort I would never have experienced the freedom I now feel. I have also learned the full meaning of gratitude, a hidden gift that has helped me never give up. My gratitude forms the base of eventually living a great life.

"Is determination born in the spirit of humans, or is it found once a passion is discovered?" I ask Olive.

"Determination is but a waste, without passion or vision. Here on these grounds of the gymnasium and Olympic birthplace are spaces for worship. Zeus inspired many. Valuable time was allowed and given to everyone to discover their dream, passion and desire."

Olive continues, "Zeus was worshipped, along with the other gods and goddesses. Each was called on for their strength, as part of the religious celebration that the Olympics began all those years ago. Zeus ignited passion in many."

"So passion is a big part of the equation. What can you tell me about finding passion?" I sit upright and listen carefully.

"When you close your eyes and see yourself as the ultimate version of yourself, what do you look like? What are you doing? Dissect this image and work backwards. You will then be shown how to achieve the ultimate version of yourself. Then your passion will be born out of your purpose. Remember to consider what natural gifts you also have," Olive encourages.

I begin my list in my head. I see myself fit, healthy and happy. I then see what needs to be done to achieve this. I see myself exercising, as well as eating properly. In the end my goal of being healthy and fit begins from my true desire to honour my body. I haven't done this in a very long time. I emotionally eat often. If a certain food tastes amazing I will always go back for a second helping. For a long time,

I've given up on looking slim and have avoided caring about it. I wondered if this is a true passion for me. I know that it is important to have passion about my body and health for it to become my reality. I realise that my own passion has to be for me first and it isn't about competing with anyone else or pleasing another. It must become my personal commitment to be worthy enough.

Placing my hand on Olive's trunk, I think about the nourishment he holds within. I know my own nourishment has to become my own priority.

I make a promise to focus on my own ultimate version of myself. I smile up at Olive and thank him. "Thank you for inspiring me by connecting me into my passion. Now I can focus on being the ultimate version of myself."

My back rests on Olive. I can do this!

CHAPTER 4

Confidence

I've been thinking back, remembering times in my life when I felt as I do today. To be confident at different times in my life, I felt like I had to 'fake it till I made it' or 'be it and then become it.' These used to be daily mantras in my life.

As a teenager I was blessed with a proportionately slim yet curvy body. I was tall and for a bit of fun I did a little bit of modelling. I sent some photos to a modelling agency and was later interviewed. I was fortunate to become part of a couple of great modelling agencies that represented some well-known international models. Because of my confidence at that time I ended up with some work under Fran Scotting Management and then with Viviens Models in Melbourne. I sometimes get out my old modelling portfolio to proudly share with my son's girlfriends now.

Back in my late teens I remember stepping into a part of myself that was a creation of the confident 'me' I wanted to be. I became it before it became me. I learned how to walk on catwalks, angle myself for photos and show up for castings. I even landed a role as an extra and stand-in for a movie with a handful of famous actors. I bumped into Guy Pearce at an airport last year, and he asked if I'd continued that type of work. I laughed as I told him my life was more about raising my four sons and working in our family construction company.

It was an exciting time back in the 80s. My memories tap into the energy of that time and the happiness I felt in being so confident. This is such a contrast to the dark time in my life later after birthing my boys, crippled for years by post-natal depression. This depression lingered until I finally remembered where my feelings grew from.

"Olive, can you tell me a little about a state of being? I've been elated, confident and happy. I've also been sad, depressed and barely surviving," I say.

"The difference between the two is never about anything external. Even if you took the most depressed person and put her in a room full of confident, happy people, her state may change slightly but not shift within. She may in fact feel inferior in a happy, upbeat place filled with smiling people. True change happens only when a switch within flicks on the light of illumination. Happiness and confidence can only replace darkness if this person stands in her own true light."

"What can a depressed person do to get rid of the horrid darkness of depression?" I ask. I have felt this struggle personally, and know how debilitating it can be.

"It always starts with a personal choice. She needs to choose her state of being first, and then become it. This allows it to become her. Fake it till you make it, I heard you think before."

My days as a model remind me that I had to first step up as if I already was a model.

"So, if someone wants to be happy they choose happiness and act happy, until happiness eventually becomes them?" I ask.

"Exactly. You, my friend, wanted confidence. Embracing strength and determination in your life, now you have stepped into who you want to be," Olive confirms.

"This is really powerful," I say with confidence. "Thank you."

"You're welcome."

Olive gives his branches a shuffle and a handful of olives fall to the ground. His gifts keep on coming.

CHAPTER 5

Passion or Obsession

When I look around at all the other olive trees in the area I know that some were purpose-planted for their symbolism of peace, endurance and, in the end, victory. They would have also been planted for to extract oil from their fruit to anoint, eat and cook with. I imagine the twisted ring of an olive branch crowning the winner of each competition. This was the symbol of victory.

Although I asked earlier, I am still unsure, so I repeat my question: "How far back where you planted here? You have already told me of being present during competitions between the Greek athletes. How old are you?" I again pry.

I have learned that the Games were part of a religious festival in honour of Zeus. The Greek Olympics began about 776 BC, later inspiring the modern Olympic Games which began in 1896. Zeus was the king of the gods, and the Olympic Games were staged every four years here at Olympia.

I can see that my friend Olive was planted at the left side of the Zeus Temple before an earthquake shook the area sometime between 520 and 550 AD. This is evident by the large stone slab that he lifted after the earthquake.

"I am over two thousand years old. I have witnessed strength, power and defeat. The earthquake broke many statues and columns, and in some areas the ground was swallowed. Many layers beneath still hold secrets of the ancients," Olive responds.

I imagine what it would have been like when the earthquake happened. Many people would have run, terrified. In my mind's eye I can see fear in their eyes as they cried out to Zeus whom they worshipped and to whom they gave sacrifice. They must have wondered what they had done wrong to cause such upheaval.

"What can you tell me about the power of Zeus? How did the people respond to the earthquake back then?" I ask.

"So many gods are celebrated for a particular

power. Zeus is above many, the leader and god of the earth. The growth of the Olympics to a worldwide phenomenon sprang from such strength. People called on the gods to gift them with some of their powers. It is no different today when people pray for help, protection or peace. Many died when the earthquake shook this area. They were terrified and thought the world was coming to an end. Those who survived re-built and renewed their faith. A while later I was deeply saddened by the fights over whose god was 'better'. The Christians dammed the ancient gods and defaced many of the stone statues. This battle started a long time ago, but still divides today."

I can feel sadness as Olive speaks. I imagine the time when war broke out and people were punished for their beliefs. I visualise the devastation of someone being told they could no longer draw strength from a god who had always provided them with strength.

I feel sad as the images tumble through my mind. I see confusion and fear in the eyes of people who believed the earthquake was an expression of anger by their god Zeus.

"Why were the Olympics started again many

years later? Was that an attempt to bring something positive back to the people of Greece?"

"It was for more than one reason. Firstly, they wanted something for entertainment. The people were great spectators. Viewing competition was good entertainment. They also wanted an activity to push themselves and achieve more physically. The Greek people were, and still are, very determined. They are strong. This resilience has always been expressed in the Olympic Games. Remember that winners were always those with drive, fuelled by the passion to be the best version of themselves," Olive tells me.

"Did you ever witness the death of someone who pushed themselves too far?" I ask.

"Yes, some people pushed themselves beyond their own limits. Obsession is different from commitment," Olive answers.

I feel what these extremes must have been like. I see similar extremes in the lives of those around me, like people who want to be thin so much that they stop eating all together.

"There's a fine line between passion and obsession," I observe.

"Your heart is the ruler of passion, while your head rules obsession. Always take note of what fuels your desires." Olive's words provide the key.

"Thank you. I have never considered this before, but I know that when I have become obsessive, it is always with my head. I've usually been shut down emotionally. I've been trying desperately to re-open my heart with the obsession of something else."

I smile and immediately think of food.

CHAPTER 6

Passion Fires Up

After time spent on the main island of Greece I board a plane full of other tourists. I've been looking forward to this part of my trip. It is time to relax and have some fun in Mykonos. I feel an excited vibe in all the other travellers on the plane. The air feels electric as we land. Some people even start clapping.

I've been travelling and having a great time with Michael my husband, but am excited that I'll also be catching up with a girlfriend from back home while I'm here.

White on white. I almost need sunglasses as I walk inside the reception at our resort. I look around at the many items –chairs, desks, couches, tables, lamps and ornaments – all white. Everything is white! At least our room has a splash of colourful cushions. The view is stunning, looking over the pool and along the coastline with its multiple moorings of million-dollar boats.

The turquoise water is warm and inviting. For a couple of days my girlfriend and I plan to do nothing but lie in the sun, swim in the pool and, most importantly, relax.

I'm immersed in my new surroundings. The resort is exquisitely beautiful. Many guests here ooze elegance, style and beauty. I can tell they have dedicated time to making their bodies toned, tanned and stylish. I feel like I'm in the wrong place, as though I've walked into the centre of a Vogue modelling shoot.

I'm surprised that here in this environment, my own sense of 'personal magic' is invoked. Has my own fire of passion been lit? Have I been inspired by seeing all these people who have taken time and care? I remember my last talk with Olive and promise to be mindful of the difference between passion and obsession.

Lying on a sunbed, I consider what I really want for my body. I put time into writing down all the aspects of what an ultimate version of myself would be. I imagine what it would be like to have all the excess, overhanging and bulgy bits of my body gone.

I share with my friend how I'm feeling and my goal to get my body back to being fit and healthy. We decide to make a pact together, determining to get fit. We commit to eating foods without sugar and dairy, and to avoiding stimulants like alcohol and caffeine. I am excited because I am looking forward to supporting each another. I know my own commitment to self-love is important for this to be possible. My friend and I both agree how incredible it would be to return here in a couple of years and not feel so misplaced.

Later in the day, in a quiet space, I make my connection back to Olive. Three breaths connect me to Olive, and I find myself sitting next to the base of my friend.

"I want to bask in your essence tonight, my friend," I say as I see myself resting my back against him. "Today I made a personal commitment and promise to bring my body back to its ultimate best. I'm sick of being overweight. I'm tired of the body pain and all the effort it takes to walk, do yoga, exercise and be active. This should all be done with ease, but it hasn't been easy for so long."

"I wondered how long it would take for you to act after I shifted a seed of passion within you,"

Olive responds.

I smile because I know that when I connect to a tree, a shift always happens in my life. I remember back to being guided into the heart-space of the beautiful Banyan when she started me on a journey to return me to the magical space of 'nothing'. I was shown a truth with Oak when she showed me the importance of choosing who I supported in my life, the amazing gift of holding space and gifting love, and the importance of balance in birds. I learned the importance of connection with Baobab when she showed me, through my own sudden disconnection with my travelling group, the importance of trusting my own instincts regarding people. This helped me discover a way to know who I wish to draw near to and who to avoid, being reminded that my tribe is important in my life. I remember how living through my heart brought joy into my life when I met with Rainbow Gum.

Now I know that by stepping forward and fully committing to Olive, I will be connecting into another new aspect of myself. I am being gifted something unique by Olive.

"Thank you for stirring and lighting this new fire within me, re-igniting my passion to be the best possible me," I say.

I feel ready and positive about my promise.

CHAPTER 7

Space Held for Loss

After several days, I leave Greece with mixed feelings. I am looking forward to sleeping in my own bed and no longer living out of a suitcase, but I know that I will be returning home to winter. I feel sad to be leaving the beautiful sunshine and clear, turquoise waters.

I fly into Athens and notice the sky is a haze-tinged red. There's an eerie feeling. I sit for a long time in transit at the airport of Athens, but no announcement is made. I have no idea what is going on. I am more focussed on preparing myself for the long 20 hours on the plane.

During the flight I struggle to get comfortable and have very little sleep.

We arrive home late in the evening. I don't unpack, instead collapsing into bed. My body is finally able to stretch out in my own bed. This feels like total luxury after having been upright for so long. I sleep solidly through the night.

By morning I notice several messages on my phone that have arrived through the night, all asking if I am safe. All over the news there are reports of several resorts just out of Athens being engulfed by an out-of-control fire. I didn't realise that yesterday's red sky was a sign of devastation all along the coast.

The news confirms that many lives were lost during a frantic attempt to escape the flames. The smoke was so thick that people became confused about which way to run for safety.

I'm reminded of the Black Saturday fires that raged out of control in the communities near our farm, back in February 2009. I remember the thick smoke and the fear that we could be in the fire's path. My boys were all young. We constantly created and revised our fire plan with strategies to stay safe.

Unfortunately, there were many people in nearby towns who weren't as fortunate. Stories of orphaned children or widowed partners shocked us all. The devastation left a scar on townships and even now, after many years, people are still trying to rebuild their lives.

There were survivors who managed to get up and dust themselves off by immediately starting to rebuild. But tragedy affects everyone differently, and sadly others were stuck in a sense of paralysing fear, loss and heartbreak. The wounded were prisoners in their own trauma.

I wonder if my friend Olive is OK and if he has been affected back in Greece. I thread my awareness toward him. A haze has made its way across the surrounding townships of Greece. Through the thin smoky haze I hold my hands against Olive and am instantly filled with a deep sadness.

Olive is the first to speak: "I feel the heartbeat of Greece as she counts the human loss. It's like a warzone, when so many innocent lives are lost all at once. I mourn not only the loss of humans, but also the damage and loss of trees."

I feel the dire mood around Olive. I cannot imagine how nature feels when trees are damaged or burnt. The only glimmer of hope that I hold for a tree is the regrowth I witnessed after the 2009 fires. Unfortunately though, some trees didn't make it. Over time I was surprised to see the new life of saplings being pushed out, through determination, from the underground root system.

I don't say anything, deciding instead to simply hold space. Together, nature and human acknowledge the loss.

As I hang my head and look toward the ground, I send love into Mother Earth. I can feel Olive doing the same.

CHAPTER 8

Commitment

Upholding my promise made in Greece, I feel committed with discipline to eat well. I embrace my new routine immediately. Olive's energy helps me and I know I am going to get results.

As soon as I clear out all the unhealthy foods from my diet, I experience a throbbing headache. I feel this for several days. I know it's caused by the withdrawal of sugar, caffeine and stimulants. My sleep is still unsettled from my jetlag. I try to embrace my detox regardless of the discomfort.

Around midday, I take a small break from working in my office and go somewhere quiet and uninterrupted where I close my eyes to settle.

I walk slowly around my friend's trunk.

"The athletes often drew strength on their

limits. It projected them further. They worked in competition with what slowed them down." Olive surprises me with this new insight.

"By looking at myself honestly it's fairly easy to see what I don't want anymore. My bulging stomach, bloated body and tight, sore, restricted joints are enough inspiration for me to give up all things that contribute to this state of being. You know, in the past I focussed on only what I wanted and this was often inspired by someone else. It was much easier to give up because I didn't know what my end result was going to be or look like. But I can work with what I focus on right now. I identify with my joints being sore, my digestion lethargic, my belly too bloated for my favourite clothes and my sleep disturbed by wakefulness. I can work with all of this. I never considered that this could motivate me." I look up at Olive. "Is there anything else that may also help?"

After a long pause Olive says in his gentle strong voice, "It's important for you to look at your reflection in the mirror each day. Not to view parts that you're unhappy with, but to also connect to your heart. Your soul resides in this part of you. Look at your reflection until you feel your personal commitment and self-love. See your beauty already present. You can be what you desire but you should always love 'you' now."

"Thank you, I'll give that a go." I understood that Olive doesn't just want me to focus on all the things I want to change in my life. He wants me to also love who I really am right now.

CHAPTER 9

Dilution of Purpose

I see ivy winding its way up Olive's trunk, and this makes me wonder if that's why a portion of his upper branches have died.

"I notice that part of you has died. Is this because ivy has made its way up your trunk?" I state the obvious. I want to know if there's a lesson for me to learn.

Olive begins to explain the relevance of this happening to him, also tapping into my own life.

"By allowing someone to have influence over your life, part of you is controlled by that person. Your purpose can be diluted by this, because it inhibits your full growth – just as you see in me," Olive shares.

I've never considered that this happens just by allowing someone influence over me. I often ask another person's opinion on whatever I'm doing at the time. I wonder if I seek someone else to help me make a decision when I doubt my thoughts. Do I give my power away each time I do this? Is my own self-doubt being stimulated by this? Perhaps I really should begin trusting my own thoughts and opinions? Many ideas spin around my mind.

"I often seek a second opinion on things that happen in my life. I didn't realise this was then diluting my purpose," I say.

"Remember when a decision needs to be made, that if it's about you or anything that is an extension of you, that weaken your own truth by asking others. You already know if you like something or not. Stick with your first impression and intuition. Then stand back and watch your ideas and creativity flourish and grow," Olive encourages.

I really like the idea of watching my hard work flourish. I have doubted my own instincts for so long that it has become second nature for me to always ask others for their opinion. I realise that over time this can take over, just as the growing ivy has begun taking over Olive.

Looking at my friend the symbolism is clear. This is what happens when I allow another person too much influence over my life.

I sit with my back comfortably leaning against Olive. I recall every time I've only made a decision after asking other person. Many of these decisions have not turned out so great. By doubting my instincts, I have been weakening my passion.

I will make the next decision for myself.

I stand beside Olive, feeling straighter and taller.

"Thank you for this insight and gift, Olive. Can I ask if you could also share your name with me? I'd really like to call you by name," I ask.

"Back when I was planted and as I grew, I was given the purpose of crowning winners in victory. My name is 'Carolos Invictus', meaning the strong 'unconquerable' or 'undefeated'."

I smile, feeling happy to know my friend Olive by his name, Carolos Invictus. "What a perfect name for you, my friend. I am so happy to be threaded to your strength, and I promise to no longer give away my power."

My hand is still on Carolos Invictus, resting solidly on a place where the ivy hasn't yet overgrown the trunk. I wish my friend had been maintained better.

CHAPTER 10

Breaking Old Habits

Emotions drag me, old habits call out my name. My perseverance and determination are diluted by temptation. I love a little sugar sprinkled through my life. I'm sure there's a way to not just make cake but eat it too. Food has been my vice for a very long time, my 'go-to' when life gets tough, confusing or unbearable.

When a little sweetness passes my lips, my smile returns and I feel pleasure. Like any addict, I love the kick the sugar gives me. I know that it's the one thing that stands in my way of a healthier body. I know my extra weight drags me down, not only on the scales but in my joints and in my bulging muffin-top belly. Then I feel the sugary smile wiped from my face.

Around I go until I stop back with my friend Carolos Invictus. I know he can help.

"Hello Rochelle," he is the first to speak.

"Morning," I say, not as chirpy as during our previous visit. "I've been doing really well with my newfound strength, perseverance and determination. But I've encountered a few hurdles lately."

"As a human, you have distractions all around. In order to survive, you have to eat. It takes time to banish old habits. Remember to also focus on what you don't want in your life. We spoke of this before," Olive encourages.

"I know I don't want to overeat or be overweight, and I don't want my clothes to be uncomfortable and tight."

"That's where you start. Each day, make your commitment against what you don't want. Do you know of anyone else who does this? Does she get results?"

"Yes, I think of other people who have achieved results. Results were difficult at first, but they have remained committed. I'm sure they still need to remind themselves why they do what they do. Every decision is filtered through what will bring the desired results," I respond.

"Today be determined to make a choice, every time you're around food. New habits will form. A new you will emerge," Olive convinces me.

My back is supported and my will is encouraged to take charge.

Closing my eyes, I soak in all of Olive's strong vibes and ponder the very fine line between victory and failure. Again, I re-commit to focussing daily on my list of what I do and don't want. Old ways, sadness, outgrown pain, habits, neglect, lack of self-love and avoidance all need to go. Beneath all that, is 'me', – vibrant, healthy, sporting a good body weight and ready to live completely happily.

Several weeks later, I notice a new determination returing and pulsing through my being. Not every thought turns to my next meal. Instead I find myself fully immersed in the activities of life. Over the weekend I ride my bike along the country roads around the farm. I feel sunshine warming my back and the sting from pushing my feet to the peddles, in muscles that haven't moved in a long time.

I also feel determined.

When I prepare and sit to enjoy my meal, I focus on fuelling my body. Past obsessions compelled me to reach for food all day long. Past emotional spikes sent me seeking sugary sweetness. No longer do I crave what will hinder the positive feeling that clean, maintained eating brings. I have so much more energy.

Slowly, I feel my body shedding the extra kilos that used to bulge over the top of my waisted clothes. In the mirror, I notice more definition. I no longer look and feel puffy.

I know that Carolos Invictus Olive's magic and gift are threaded into my life. His many offerings have changed the way I am able to show up in my life.

Parts of me, once broken, are now restored and made whole.

"Meeting you, Carolos my friend, has been the very thing I needed and that I had missed in my life for so long. I no longer feel that I've given up on myself. Your essence of determination is infused into all that I do in my life."

I hold my hand to the thick bark of Olive.

"Your spirit can achieve anything it wishes," Olive congratulates me, before continuing. "From the very core of every dream you wish, comes your own personal part to play. Play hard and give it everything. Live your life with passion as if you already have reached your goals."

I knew exactly what Carolos meant.

CHAPTER 11

Embracing Change

I sit enjoying the silence of Olive for a little while.

I hear and see birds as they flutter around the area. Many musical tones make a beautiful chorus. I notice that there's a variety of birds here at Olympus.

I remember what my friend Oak told me about birds being the only animal that lived on earth but flew in the sky. It is while they glide up above that they are at peace. Gracefully birds have the ability to be active and busy, and then able to relax and glide through the sky. This reminded me of what it was like to meditate and how important it is to have this same contrast in my own life.

"Birds are a great example of the balance needed," I say.

"Yes, they are. I am also an example of how to gain balance. The seasons gift me a time for new growth, bearing fruit, dropping my leaves and being dormant." Olive draws another parallel.

I respond: "I have always been fascinated by the cycles of life. I draw on these in my own life. In spring I like to manifest who I want to be. The list of what I really want to become is like this. I know what I don't want and, just like you when you shed leaves, I let go of these things. The heat of summer helps also to burn away all that is no longer required in my life. The dormant time of winter is a great time to be still and really consider life. In winter I love to rug up and nurture myself. Is this the same for trees?"

"Absolutely. Trees have times of great change. Nothing ever remains the same. Night is different from day, seasons change the temperature and the energies all around. I have witnessed extremes. You should always embrace change. When everything stops changing it also stops growing and evolving," Carolos says.

"You remind me that my journey will always be something new. I will always have opportunity to change as well. I am forever grateful for meeting you and being infused with determination and perseverance which have resulted in a newfound confidence. I embrace all that my life can be," I conclude.

"Remember to share my gifts, Rochelle. Remember to never give up on you."

These are the final words spoken.

Silence blankets this space in time, boundless and eternal. I know I am seeded and have forever been threaded with the strength to confidently be 'me'.

I stand and lean my back up against my friend Olive, Carolos Invictus, a giant earth tree that has gifted me with the right to begin living the life I should.

Also by Rochelle

Banyan Tree Wisdom: My Gift to You
Banyan Tree Wisdom: Wisdom Cards
Meeting Rosie Banyan:
Learning Forgiveness, Trust and Love
I Give You My Word: Journal

EARTH GIANT TREE GIFT SERIES
(GIFT BOOKS & AUDIO BOOKS)

Book 1: Oak Tree's Gift
Book 2: Baobab Tree's Gift
Book 3: Banyan Tree's Gift
Book 4: Rainbow Gum's Gift
Book 5: Olive Tree's Gift
Book 6: Pagoda Tree's Gift

ALCHEMY OILS

Banyan Tree: 'Restore Balance', 'Dream',
'Release' & 'Beauty Wisdom Power'
Oak Tree: 'Truth'
Baobab Tree 'Connection'
Banyan Tree 'Balance'
Rainbow Gum 'Joy'
Olive Tree 'Confidence'
Pagoda Tree 'Clarity'

www.treevoice.global

About the Author

A busy business owner, wife and mother, Rochelle thrived in the corporate and finance world in her early adult years. Then, after her fourth son, a wave of postnatal depression debilitated her, forcing her to re-visit the horrors of her sexually abusive childhood. With grit and determination she laboured against her own broken past and breathed life back into her shutdown heart, cracking open its language and capturing it in writing. She learned to trust in the universal soul path she'd stepped onto.

Each time she experienced a healing method that helped her, Rochelle became qualified in that field to then help others. She became a Bowen Therapist, Reiki and Seichem Master, Clinical Hypnotherapist using NLP methods, Journey Worker and Intuitive Healer. She also owned and ran a Day Spa and Healing Centre in North East Victoria.

Rochelle now immerses herself in connections with nature as they flow, bringing to life the lessons and messages through writing, speaking and facilitating. Her journey has led her to many parts of the globe. She has pitched to Hollywood in New York; she has hosted women's retreats in Bali; she has learned from poverty-stricken leaders in Senegal Africa; and she discovered the 'simple' life in Vanuatu.

Rochelle's message is honest, raw and authentic, and her words are greatly needed as we all navigate our next chapter here on earth.

AUTHOR, SPEAKER, ALCHEMIST,
A LOVER OF NATURE AND
VIBRANT LIVING

Connect with Rochelle

hello@treevoice.global

www.facebook.com/TreeVoiceAuthor

www.facebook.com/RochelleHeverenAuthor

Instagram: @treevoiceglobal

Instagram: @rochelle_with_love_x

www.treevoice.global

www.ingramcontent.com/pod-product-compliance
Lightning Source LLC
Chambersburg PA
CBHW032049290426
44110CB00012B/1020